Rhapsody in D

Rhapsody in D

by

Todd Bruce

Turnstone Press

Turnstone Press
607–100 Arthur Street
Winnipeg, Manitoba
Canada R3B 1H3

Turnstone Press gratefully acknowledges the support of
the Canada Council for the Arts and the
Manitoba Arts Council for our publishing program.

The Canada Council | Le Conseil des Arts
FOR THE ARTS | DU CANADA
SINCE 1957 | DEPUIS 1957

Cover art: Lynda Blanchard

Design: Manuela Dias

This book was printed and bound in Canada by
Friesens for Turnstone Press.

Canadian Cataloguing in Publication Data

Bruce, Todd, 1965–

Rhapsody in D

Poems.
ISBN 0-88801-211-X

I. Title.

PS8553.R8223R42 1997   C811'.54   C97-920026-1
PR9199.3.B7383R42 1997

*This book is dedicated to the memory of
Dr. Dan M. Wilmot (1945-1995)
because he lived through it with me
and because I wrote it for him.*

Acknowledgements

My sincere thanks to the Manitoba Arts Council for making this publication possible.

I would also like to thank Rob for always saying "I want more," Debbie for helping me to understand what I was writing, Dawne for uncovering masked voices, Robert Kroetsch & Dennis Cooley for offering me fresh (but not clean) pages, Mark for his quiet, patient consideration, Jamie for his keen eye and erotic delay, and Bill for coming up with the perfect title.

Table of Contents

Rhapsody (ræ psodi), *sb.* 1542 [- L. *rhapsodia*, applied by Cornelius Nepos to a book of Homer, - **1.** An epic poem or part of one, suitable for recitation at one time. †**2.** A miscellaneous collection; a medley or confused mass (*of* things); a 'string' (*of* words, sentences, tales, etc.) - 1837. †**b.** A literary work consisting of miscellaneous or disconnected pieces; a written composition having no fixed form or plan - 1764. †**c.** A collection (*of* persons, nations) - 1701. **3.** An exalted expression of sentiment or feeling; an effusion (e.g. a speech, letter, poem) marked by extravagance of idea and expression, but without connected thought or sound argument. **4.** *Mus.* An instrumental composition enthusiastic in character but of indefinite form - 1880.

A singular chorale, made piece by piece, one flower of vocal polyphony, another flower, then another, their suite not making a melodic intrigue, each one sufficing for itself in the internal comparison of voices, the suite only being constructed afterward, to make a whole.

—Jean-François Lyotard

What Happens When Someone
Recalls a High-Wire Act That Failed
Without a Net

One of these days I'll fall. Free fall. Perhaps I'll survive.

And then I am on the train, staring out across the landscape, letting it survive. And then my naked body across a cold stone floor. And then I pull my silver flask from my pocket and enjoy a cocktail, a smoke.

(I never thought I'd come to this), wiping sweat from my brow because of you.

If I was in it, I could blame it all on love.

I challenge the night to transform into dawn, whisky slung from my wrist, whisky rising with the sun & a spilling from the vacancy of your eyes. Spit trickling from my tongue as I fall (and then) into sleep. The train car I'm in . . . being pulled . . . along the undulating prairie. Flat, my ass.

I'm in the bar car, under the skylight, drinking Bloody Marys, and you think you can tell me about the stars, about Northern Lights as though they were exotic. And I let you take me into the story, take me out of the poem. Tell me I say.

I'm under the skylight, in the bar car, drinking Drambuie,
studying the colour of a blood orange. I remember how
concise it was when I caught it in my palm, and the smile on
your lips. I was afraid to slice it open, to close by opening.
By now, its colour has deepened, deeper than your eyes can
see. Its skin is almost thin enough to expect it to dry into
something health stores sell to treat bulging eyes. I'm certain
you've thought of all its implications. And then you tell me
you have passed a dew-sopped rose into the hand of a
princess at the moment dawn flares (like music) (or a cat
paw) over the horizon.

Near the rear there is a car full of chalk slates. You might say
they are in transit.

I am still and I listen to my breathing (my eyes are out at the
stars), the train moves coyly through foothills. I am waiting
for my lungs to collapse. And then to cross a bridge and to
derail into a river. And then to swim and to kiss the
enchanted reed's roots and to escape gold-lipped and bubble-
blowing, shy like a virgin prince.

But I implore you, be absolutely silent. The curtain is white
and sheer and it billows into the room, above my
amphibious eyes.

I often wonder when I will begin to miss you.

You, in a fresh clearing, your knees drawn up under your
chin, your eyes staring in the direction I left. Empty, oil-
stained popcorn boxes and burst balloons roll in the wind
around you. The sun has long since set and you light a
cigarette. In the hour before dawn, the ground blows a mist,
or it is smouldering. Your hair is being tossed a little.

The memory of a Ferris wheel, turning in the theatre of your mind.

Water, or its tide, tugging off my shoes. I am sad. And I am staring into the blur of a candle flame. The candle being green and the room being scented with beeswax. But then, of course, I am only alive in recollection, in the infirmary of recollection.

But then again it isn't as though I've confessed to having begun.

And these words might pull you through, for all I know, these words might turn into a hand that reaches up and out of the page to pinch into the vibrating flesh of your red red heart. (Or blue in a pane of glass). The rhythm might change the beat. Or, more likely, we will dream of one another and find in the oxbow of our river an illimitable desire for distinction, or the desire to remain, to remain, as other than.

He sings to me, to us, "lift up your hearts." The church is cold and the church is warm.

I remember fumbling into my first step, I remember blood on the kitchen floor, I remember drinking the Monkey's Lunch and I remember falling asleep saying I am tired, I love you, I am tired.

I reach to feel your smouldering skin or the bubble of blood that winds (you are in ribbons) across your shaking, marrow-sopped bones. I stretch out my self in longing and in utter senselessness, an ecstasy.

Once, I remember forgetting you.

I remember wanting you to share a new-found ecstasy, I remember rage spitting in my lungs and then I remember understanding this unsharability, this oneness, this aloneness, this republic of the self.

And I should cup your tear-streamed face in my hands and look you in the eye and I will make a pass of words be seen from my lips and they will billow around your trembling head and I will let you read the sky on which is written I shall never have cause to war with you again.

Descant

"Every act is a translation."

I have split the skin on my face for diving into an empty
pool.

A burning tobacco advances toward my lips and blueless
smoke (a cringing, clear sky) clings to my cheek and glides
across my squinting eye. An ash drops and sparks on my lap.
I brush it away. And today the seeds began to fall. An acorn
storm like a rain and the earth springs open its eyes,
sparrows popping green seeds into their ashen beaks. And
not one oak will grow in this control, it is best to plant, and
yet they dance or storm or drape and wail and exhale . . . dot
dot dot be furrowing insolent dramatic precise covalent true
a sleeping crying, a crying, a cry a weeping to sleep. A
whisky might slip to my lips and be drunk.

you, with breath

You are a bird whose hunger remains in the traffic of your
tree-lined streets. Winter's coming and already it's been long
and hard. Your body is oily and slick and a blood-feather has
been hacked and scabbed and muffled. You have young to
feed and a song to sing and you have foxes to look out for.
You have properties you will not sell and wisdom none will
buy. You are my archangel with a long and slender trumpet.
You resuscitate the snapdragon with a song. A humming-
bird delights in giving nectar back to her flower.

*You must win the race by cheating, must lie to say you have had
words with God.*

Yes, you, my hero, the most beautiful of all fallings, I will
pray for you when you are gone. I will wait for the moment
we reunite. I, an empty staff, a stringless cello, an armless
pianist. Will you fall for me? Will you tumble and bleed and
curse the sky? Can you empty yourself and die prideless and
full of sorrow? Will you wilt like a rose who has never seen
the sun?

A window separates us
between life and death

can't watch you leave me, heartstring
can't watch you skip like a stone

on clear black water
you (up) stroke your paddles like straws
(down) sipping

entice me as you
will me to sing

gardens

A woman in a print dress, daisies blue & shattering giants a
gold. She carries a white cardboard box in her arms, across it
is written "*dimanche*" and she is pulling the tops (the flowers)
of weeds from off their stems. She gardens the grounds of
the church and screeches like a crow at the ringing of her
bells.

She thinks about words like garden and stone. She thinks
about stained glass eroding into plates. She thinks she must
concentrate on potential demise. She moves like a wind has
touched her thousands of years ago.

She drinks dandelion wine and sits at her painting. A mad clown pokes his finger out of the canvas and he is trying to dig into her flesh. She dabs her brush into a dune of burnt umber and empties her glass. It is vendredi and she looks west (out her kitchen window) to the sky beginning to split into ribbons.

As though she lives again.

(but)

He moves onto the bed and places a cool damp cloth across his eyes. He reaches to the side-table and fumbles for a cigarette. He recalls in an instant all of his darkest and most secret pleasures. He blows long trains of smoke across his naked body, exhaling himself into the night. He remembers the end of a story, he remembers when we die we become stars, our first glowing, perhaps, a millennium from your eyes.

Will you become
my heartstring
a star?

I remember you remembering a shadow of a shadowless ghost, remembering the shadow of water. I remember you forgetting to remember. I remember you remembering you cannot remember. Do you remember me remembering you not remembering?

I'm so scared of you making me real that sometimes I cry. Sometimes I cry. And when I cry I rehearse the unreal, I say to you, wherever you are, I say this to you.

Things get this way you know. Convoluted, I convolute the forgotten memory of you.

Some day soon, I will stub you out, like a cigarette. Paint a cross over my heart with cinders.

The flower part

I have brought roses (wild, yellow & wild) meant for you. To
the sucklings of cows. And they have wet them and left
them. Be withdrawn from their hunger, quaking blossoms
like teats, refused.

But then, of course, I have flowers.

Water

And here I am, at the end of your words, rain in my eyes,
tears falling to the thirsty earth, and I am smudging oil
paints across a beginning, a beginning like an end, a
beginning as though you had never intended to see me
watch you close and there is rain, like a wedding when your
story ends. These might be the words of my raining like a
flood. On the new horizon we swim to one another, burning
like oil spills, flickering rainbows in mud puddles. And as I
paint this tree branch, sunlight changes as though suns are
innumerable and coexistent, as though, for an instant, our
love has come alive. And then I am stooping with a sweating
drink in hand, clamouring into the sky on moon symbols
and deploying the arsenal of my desire into the bloody and
strangled universe of your sigh. If the text could cry, my
love, these pages would *never* be turned.

But in the sweet raw morning we are incomplete like a
howling, the moon is chalk on the premature sky and spit on
your tongue evaporates as you utter your poem or relinquish
your clothes to suck on the dew.

     do not die for me but eclipse my eye
       send me beggars and their cupped hands shall brim with
gold
       drink the pebbles of water from an iris bowl
       scent the air between us with your tongue

You tell me this has nothing to do with sacrifice and the days of love have never come, you tell me. You tell me love is improbable. And you tell me this as you sit naked in a cage of bullrushes, the sky limited and parabolic above you. And if it were to rain we would disregard the need for symbolism. Love has no symbols, you say, no language no need no material. I call to the dawn, dreaming of the moon we do not howl to. I say you tell me lies.

The train has stopped. Last night, under the skylight, the waiter told me it would. But this is not my stop, it is here that I will not arrive. The waiter is at my cabin door, in his dungarees and sweatshirt, his face has darkened with a morning-full of whiskers and his shoulder carries the weight of a hockey bag, in his hand is a suitcase he borrowed from an aunt. He seems sad I shan't disembark, he seems sad at the drink in my hand. The waiter is sad at me often, when the day is lighted by the sun. He tells me he has no choice but to leave, to be here, to register for university. The waiter was sure I would be coming off the train with him, as though he thought I might recognize the importance of the city in which he lived. Frankly, I told him, I haven't a clue where we are. I shall wait for the train to begin again.

Would you care to kiss me good-bye?

What fools boys can be, bursting with love. How ceremoniously romantic. The greatest of all combinations, piety and hormones.

Finally, he is gone. Remember me he said and already I have forgotten his name. I have been wondering what is wild this year in your rock garden. I am dreaming a picture of your favourites. Double-headed daisies and black-eyed Susans. I am wondering if you still keep dragonflies. I suppose though you have never lost your taste for wild honey. Isn't it strange that I remember you forgetting yourself? How long did you live without ever knowing me? Do you know this verb to unlearn? Ah, the rain has begun again and it speaks to me through the skylight. Can you listen for it through these words?

Time has streamlined itself and just as the train begins to pick up momentum a woman enters the bar car, shaking a yellow umbrella and smoothing her hair. She is polite in smiling at me but prefers to be seen by the waiter. She impresses me by ordering vodka rocks. I have guessed her name but prefer to be silent and self-distracting. What is that line about sweet chicory?

She tells me first what I already know, her name. I know, I say, my eyes turned down toward my book. She tells me I am a liar; more of what I already know. Thank you, I say. She sits down across from me uninvited and tells me how impossible it is that I should know her name. After all, we have never met. She says she is from Brazil (Braseel). As she turns her head to get the attention of the waiter, I glance at her. She dresses in yellow and I wonder if she has an umbrella for every outfit. Her complexion is brown. Her hair is black. The plush red velvet of the armchair is inhaling her. At a glance, she is very beautiful, but beauty has become a sense for her and it strikes me as a casual bore. I tell her it has been a long time since I have made love to a woman.

The scene ends very expensively, my eyes stinging with vodka, and her licking it from my lips.

We are both holding cigarettes in historical poses and the waiter brings by a round of drinks. He has run out of my preferred Scotch and apologizes. This place can grow trees tall enough to be seen from my seat. Where I was born, trees stand as misplaced commas, where I was born, and it frightens me to think I have left. Tricky, don't you think? Nonetheless, she is uninspired but then again inspiration, necessarily, cannot be fleeting.

I can only, faithfully, credit it as inevitable companionship; law according to Hobbes. Thus, we simultaneously broke our fasts in the barely tolerable absence of honeydew. At times I even removed my wristwatch. We shared quips from our respective readings over two-hour lunches, departed into afternoon naps, and dressed for dinner. She told me once, over aperitifs, that her entire family was killed at an outdoor musical concert. She said they were stormed with perfection. With smoke slowly being exhaled she told me she respected them all for the way they died. She regrets, she tells me, her inability to hear. But then she asked me, secretly, where would I be departing. And I blew out a fraction of smoke and whispered with shifting eyes that I am not.

I am not about to begin re-reading you, angered as I am. I toss you aside to crack your spine. I am too compelled to misunderstand myself, too trustworthy of your failings. All I feel I can do is sing to you. I, I, I, have mishappened into this your truth and forever I shall wonder . . .

Tell me, I might say, if you were here, what it means to be a body hanging from a tree. You are so pretentious, she says, scribbling away and whooshing your eyes up to the stars. She tells me I strike her as a fraud. Such a fool, such an emotional thing you are, she says to me and laughs and crushes out a cigarette. I am only teasing, she recants, quite frankly, I think it's adorable, you, pretending to be a poet. But I tell her, I am no such thing.

I think I am probably quoting someone when I say that when we run away from that which gives us pain, we eventually run into it again. And did I tell you that the new waiter is particularly boring? I have set the chess board in my cabin. I have been pondering my first move for days. Shall we enjoy a match on the patio when I return?

She tells me that my dress is boring. She so often refers to me as "boring." Thank you I say. I tell her I can not imagine how unlucky she must feel to have found me here. How sorry she must be there are no others. There is no piano aboard this train. Tell me, she says, what was I to expect? So I read to her from my book. I have not stopped reading it since I began. I believe it has never begun, can never end, the ink, in places, has run with my sweat. In response she shows me a photograph of her family on the evening of their death.

And the train moves on (a diamond-chipped needle following its groove) and I wonder how many pennies we have rolled across or silver dollars under electrician's tape. Or how many children we rumbled over clinging like spiders to an iron web.

You might say I am going nowhere and you may be correct. Or you might wonder, am I coming home to you? I may or may not be aware of the direction I follow. Perhaps I shall dream of you soon, giving you freedom to be in my future. For now, this potential must suffice. For now, you are safer at a distance. This idea of stasis in motion I know interests you, this idea of the memory of forgetting. But I am doing all the things I have longed to do. I am moving and moving is enough, but before I left I hung the wind chimes you sent to me outside my bedroom door. We live our lives as randomly as notes struck from the touch of their ivory tongues. Can we love as neatly as that, should I meet with you again? Should I tell you I am wearing the sweater you love, the one you patched while I slept like a cat in your sun-room? Or should I tell you I would have cried into your arms the night you taught me how to fly?

I am in my cabin and the sun is rising toward my window. A tear drizzles down the curve of my nose because I have not slept. But soon I will pull closed the blind and slumber, knowing the moon has passed without event.

In the beginning the train was stopped, spinning its wheels on ice and snow.

I have pulled shut the blind and have re-become.

Slowly I lose the purpose of time.

Quickly(,) I am.

touching the running shadow of you

watching you through the spaces

of my fingers

brief and cool

a sip

spit on a hot iron

it causes me to cry

to watch you not become

She lights a cigarette (the fluorescence expanding, flickering the shadow behind her). Shaking her head, she exhales smoke in a sigh (snaps shut the flame of the match with a flick of her wrist) and reminds me of my vulnerability. As she waves her hand (and this) for a drink, I tell her I am none of the things she thinks I may be. And then she leans across the table, a vodka martini dangling from her ruby-ringed fingers, and whispers.

(and whispers)
and she whispers
I am hiding you

Have I told you the leaves have begun to fly and that I miss
the blatancy of the prairie sky?

It is mysterious and somehow I suspect labyrinthine in design,
these words growing of their own accord, or was it you who
slipped into my room and composed this poem for me?

But there is no trace of your scent withdrawing through the
crack of the window or escaping from the door.

Rather prophetic wouldn't you say? But I know all too well you will laugh and shake your head in mild disappointment at my misunderstanding. Your metaphors, you will say, are my reality, your status quo, my illusion. You will wait for me to arrive and sit me down outside the garden, and as you weed and dig and divert you will whisper the truth to me once again. You will tell me there is no such thing as magic. Magic is for the dreamers. There is magic around us all the time, your reality is senseless to it. That is all. What you see as magic is not magic, what you see as magic is what is. And then you will tilt your head toward the garden and it will begin to grow as if in time-lapse, and we will hear the leaves stretching and aching and the roots protruding. We will see flowers bloom and die and seed and bloom and die and seed and bloom and die again in seconds and you will say to me that I believe that this is magic, that I will say this contradicts the laws of nature, that I will say this is an exception to the rule. And then you will open the green and orange colours of your eyes and ask me to tell you what the world is all about. And I will say that I know nothing and you will answer that this is not true. You will say to me, tenderly, you know, at least, that you do not know. "Come let us speak of other things and boil this root into some tea." It thrusts itself like a web through the openings of your gently clutching hand.

And I am sipping blackberry tea and I remember how you taught me to stir it with sugar and milk and to blow slowly over its steaming surface. Isn't that, I wonder, what your memory of me is like? And the waiter, perplexed with me, refills my tea pot from his silex of boiling water until its flavour is washed away. Somehow, as if I might blame it on autumn, I am disenchanted by the reality of loss. But the train is slowing to a stop again and I signal the waiter to pour me a Scotch.

I think this is the word you were attempting to say,
"extraordinary." And then that my extraordinary is your
ordinary, but that you never allow it to be defined. I think, for
now, you might say that for every thing we define, a piece of our
world crumbles away. And this is when you laugh and answer
with your eyes, they might be saying "ah, you are defining the
greatest of all binaries, you speak of the say and of the do." Once
you told me it would be all right if we all remembered to stop. And
then you regretted having said it is midnight, minutes before . . .

The train is to depart again and into the bar car he enters.
He nods at me as I look over the rim of my emptying
highball. He smiles and moves forward with his hand
extended and asks if I am the man he is to meet. And as I
look around me I wonder if six months from now I will be
methodically ripping the pages from *By Grand Central
Station I Sat Down and Wept* and tossing them like playing
cards into a fire I built in a home I rented for lack of any
other while getting drunk. But instead I say, no, I don't think
so.

Mmmm is love who dashes away in the swoop of a cape. Are you
sitting on the porch and leaning forward out of your chair so that
the juice from the nectarine (cracking between your lips) will drip
between the slats of wood beneath your feet? Do you smile, your
lips humming with gnats? Do you wait for a flashing
thundershower to wash away the nectar of her womb? Or have you
crept into your library to search for the secrets of wooden seeds?
How I wish I were there, watching you laugh into the open mouth
of an unwashed sun. You might tell it that its tongue is black . . .

But the story has removed itself for fear of me, has slithered
away like light under a closing door, has gone stalk still like a
bird whose bill resembles a woody reed, and I wait for it to
panic in my long and slender silence, or it waits for me (an
absent idea).

But I am its crow (dear) in early spring, I am hunting for that which has not been laid, or that which has not been shed, or I have come early to sacrifice myself to the barren soil (can you push me through this marsh or walk me over it on webbed and patient stilts), to be seen clearly against the fading snow or be the first to walk the ungiving high-wire against the melting and slobbery sky.

And when spring might arrive, you told me, crow will walk across the sky. And if he finds that the world is near to death he will caw and caw in his glee (mischievous as he is), but because of his noise, bear shall awake from her sleep and scratch the belly of the earth until it too awakes and begins to renew. And then the crow will caw again as though he is pleased and he will eat.

But these are dreams now or the colour is retreating from my memory. And I have come to a halt, and I sit and I walk with a noticeable lean. I have ordered fruits for my lunch and a bottle of champagne. The sounds of peeling fruit will always remind me of you. The waiter is wiping the dust from his crystal highballs and he shakes his head at me as I drop wedges of lemon and orange into my flute glass and laugh to myself and drink. I ask him to bring me cigarettes with brightly coloured papers, cigarettes with gold insignia and tobacco that tastes of a lazy sun and then I tell him I would like to hear Beethoven's late string quartets. Finally, he smiles and looks to the stones who glare at him as we pass them. He walks toward me and soundlessly removes the cellophane from a package of John Player Specials and places one between my teeth. But as he walks away, clicking shut his lighter (coloured like ivory), I remind him of the pleasures of grapefruit.

I am dreaming and I am on my back in a field of flax, their heads are full of eyes rocking over me and chanting. I see a whisky-jack land in a lone and leafless birch (funny I think, a jack away from its home) and above it, through the failing tree, the moon is a bracket closing)

the moon is
   sliced
        into the raven's tail
      last flicker of night

the trees smell
faintly of age

(. . . hibernation . . .)

     the smell peeling out from under your balls

Shhh

   October's eye hovers

      quietly and blinks

& the reds

Startle from out the mountain ash

while birches sneer pale uprisings

and a blue jay shudders inside a strict jack pine
a feather she has discarded
loops to the ground and she squawks

her black eyes dilating
into accusing periods

as though her young have fallen
(.)open-beaked(.)
to the treacherous forest floor

I dreamed of you again in your rock garden. Do you remember in the sun-room was a map of the lakes and like crocus petals they bloomed a cartographer's bloom? My finger falls into its centre and its touch constricts the ventricle I might be to you. And I sit and watch you (my knees pulled tight beneath my chin) while you dig and tuck beneath your bandanna a loose tress of hair. The flower-patterned gloves across your hand wipe sweat from your brow and you cleanse your infant garden of weeds and stones and sticks and dried blossoms and a dead baby chipmunk and can tabs and bottle tops and some hosiery and the memory of your brothers who have died and then you mist the bud of the wild yellow rose and smile like a child and it has been many years since you uttered the word "mother."

The train (with me inside it) is passing through a curving descent in the middle of the night, and the skylight proves to me that the earth is padded with layers of thick and thirsting clouds and that the rain is sprinkling out from them but has yet to touch the ground. The man with extended hand has been searching for hours for the man he was to meet. He enters and exits the bar car with the frequency of fear and finally sits down next to a window and orders a dark and bubbling drink. He is distressed and lonely and scratches the under-chin of his speckled beard. He takes a long pull on his drink and loosens his tie. As I watch the veins in his forehead relax, I pull from my breast pocket a cigarette and snap fire into its eye. Several cocktails later he yells to me across the room. He asks me what I am reading and I pretend I haven't heard. He asks louder and I ignore him again. The waiter takes a deep breath and stifles a knowing sigh. The man with extended hand walks toward me with his drink. I look up at the instant he says I was talking to you. I reach into my coat pocket, it is draped across the chair next to me, and pull out an ocarina. I put its string over my head and begin to play an ancient love song for him and he is astounded and sits across from me and orders me a drink. He is drunk and asks if I am the man he was to meet. I put the ocarina to my lips and I play until he has sobbed away his anger, I play until he confesses his love for me.

He is lies, all lies, and he tells me he plays the harpsichord. When he opens his mouth I see crocuses that grow in the lining of his throat. I see buttercups blooming in the V of his neck, and when he looks me in the eye I see the petals of daisies like tangents from his glossy and contracted pupils. Blue lobelia spill out from the cuffs of his starched white shirt (and I imagine his fingers running across the keys), fanning up a scale and I wish his name to be Mathias, but I know it is not. He is a perfumed murmur and I wonder if he can be resisted.

In the morning, at breakfast, I excuse myself from the table to wash my hands. He remarks at my "politeness" and I nod with a frown and sneak into my cabin to take your queen by sacrificing my bishop. You are lost, I know, without your queen but your uncharacteristic risk was too much for me to ignore. This morning, my bishop touches your robe with hands sticky from the sugar of an orange.

I am collecting your fallen men into a manila envelope, I shall mail them to you when I reach a post. Perhaps I should accompany them, perhaps I always have. But you do not have to tell me, your begonias are visions to behold and you have recently tied the knot of the last stitch in your double wedding ring quilt. I shall ask you when I arrive how it is that "self" for you is a community. I shall ask you about the secrets of the perfection of the beautiful. And I will ask you to remind me of the impossibility of beauty. I will listen to you tell me that beauty is process.

The man with the extended hand is looking in the direction of the door through which I enter. He says he thought I got lost. My body contorts into the shape of a question mark and swells and deflates, quickly, as though it is also exclaiming. So I tell him that I did. He tells me he is a "therapist" and that what I need is to make love.

But he has hypnotized me and the walls of the bar car collapse and the skylight, my skylight, explodes toward the stars and then he brings me a spectacular plum and he smells of lilac and sandalwood. Amethysts stud every finger of his extended hand and the plum is on a silver tray and he places it on my lap and he closes the cabin door and then begs me to let him watch me eat.

I was shameless in my nudity and the stickiness of my lips. I could not bear the thought of the moment of love, the beauty removing itself from its process, the phrasing of that desire eluding its irresistible continuity of line. Oh it would have made you laugh out in happiness. You will be laughing out in happiness now. Have I told you I love you like flowers love the rain? Like a seed its fruit, a child its womb? Do you understand what it means for me to be offered a plum, the colour of its flesh so surprising beneath its purple skin? I have saved its pith to plant in your garden of wild and yellow roses. Under its tree we shall return.

I slept for six days, four hours, twenty minutes and seventeen seconds. I was hungry and thirsty and he was gone. The waiter served me eggs and muffins and apple juice with coffee. And when I was fed he explained to me that the man with the extended hand had departed when he realized he was moving east and had wanted to be going west. I offered the waiter a fifty dollar bill for a bottle of Scotch and solitude. And as I took my first drink I noticed on the hand tipping toward my eyes a ruby set in gold and I wondered how romantic I must seem, living this life of oxymorons.

29

And then I am on the train and you think you can ask me why it is I need to love. And I wonder at the poverty of your soul. And then I tell you that I wonder if you have mis-spoken "love" for "live."

I am in the bar car and because the sun is so exact I am drinking Jack Daniels and I am pencilling question marks into the margins of the book you barely remain in. And then I remember how we made love, never touching.

And I will bring to you the seeds of an English daisy (she who covers her eyes in the absence of the sun), and petals of India ink so that you may paint me naked on a rock.

& I will bring myself to you, a closed gentian. But you are where water runs and I am racing toward it with wine in my blood, hunger inside my belly and ruin upon my soul. But you . . . you fall away from me or we move in opposite directions burning with blind desire one for the other, but time is curved and eventually we shall unite.

If the truth be told, I was born a word, and I search for it in you. I rummage through your language or pull myself down and away from the surface of its lake.

Like snowberries
my (eyes) turn
inward and long
to be fed upon.

I am absolutely controlled by symmetry and the idea of the line. I am moved by the unconscious desire to fail, and to see collapse around me your fortress of words. Can you love a man so devilish as to blow away at the briefest gust of the wind? Who are you? Or how is it so that you are?

It has rained for twenty-eight days (but I need you like the flowers need the sun) and the whites of my eyes reflect the grey bellies of the clouded sky. In my mind I transpose the movements of your body onto the strings of a jester's lute and you are alive again in the asylum of my memory. And then the waiter offers me an icy drink and a raku black vase full of bluebur and narrow-leaved puccoon and when I remember the forgotten man with extended hand the sky outside begins to glisten with the pouring of rubies and the earth rubs her belly with thanks, or perhaps with greed.

Dawn (the light who makes the statues sing) has entered like the ringing of a bell and I awake to her like a fish being unhooked and returned to the water. Finally the glow of the sun, finally the possibility of beginnings.

The flowers are bitter and resent the sun. For a moment, the flowers have forgotten. The flowers will fight their sun. The flowers have grown thick and unwilling to shed their life-preserving armour. And seventy-six years will pass before the flowers make peace with the sun. Somewhere a woman teaches her children that beauty, strength and weakness are one.

Can you see the sound of light? Can you hear the vetchling expel her breath?

The pollen of the lilies you left me is the colour of rust and has stained the palm of my hand.

I am smothered with floral images, drunk with nectar, and I am romantic.

Am I beginning to answer your questions?

The motion of the train confronts me like a hangover and I take longer than usual to bathe and dress. I wear my best trousers and a jacket and tie. I have polished my shoes and my belt and my fingernails are shiny and trimmed. Dinner is being served as I enter the dining car, but I see you immediately and my heart begins to race. The waiter has kept my table open, but is tactless in noting my appearance. I make it clear to him that nothing less than a triple Scotch will suffice. My hands are shaking as I turn open my book and look into it. I have crossed my legs just so and my cigarette is perfect. I instruct the waiter to bring me a perfectly cooked top sirloin with wedges of orange and fresh strawberries. With it will arrive a glass of long flat red that I have not ordered. I send it away with a note saying how surprised I am that you have not noticed I am drinking Scotch and my belief that long flat red should only be drunk just before dawn. With the Scotch comes a note asking me to forgive you. How excellent and temporary seems my control, how perverse the timing. And later that night with your legs wrapped around mine I will know it is love that destroys. And sipping wine, we watch the sunrise from the cabin window, and I brush the first spark of its light from the corner of your eye.

In momentary sprees of sanity, I attempted to limit the relationship. I tried to speak of my vulnerabilities. We were like two hydrogen atoms trying to unlearn their instinctual alliance with oxygen. And so I waited for the force to come which would disengage us like fire. Such a fool, you are saying and wagging your head, such a fool am I that you will put this letter aside without reading it and leave it to tend your garden. Harvest is less than a moon away and the mud room is singing to you with the echo of empty honey jars.

Piper

I was thinking (about thinking) that he could make the pipes sing. Trumpets crashing and crushing their bleats through them, pianos rolling up their bright brass bellies and rattling out their valves, harps floating up and down and never out them, piccolos being shy in them, fanning their eyes in them, in this parade (I was thinking) he could make the pipes sing sounds the likes of which cast upon your heart a burden of love too great to bear, too powerful to resist and you know you can sing as the lips of your red red mouth stretch out and open into an O.

I was singing (my deepest song): unpin me mother and let me sing.

I have seen the piper (his eyes so bright) stretch his lips about the end of an eave and I have seen him blow through it and I have seen dried poplar leaves tossed like ashes in a flurry from your rooftop and I have seen the piper buried in blood. I have seen a garter snake swallow a robin's bright blue egg. A robin's egg bright and blue.

The piper sings for the beginning of time, to herald the never told, to share the story you've been waiting for. And the piper is twitching his eyes and lapping his tongue and the piper has wet the reed of your soul and the piper is flown high above the blood-spotted earth, clawed through the spine by a bird from whose waste dangles the embers of remembrance, and he sings and he plays all the songs you have known, and then he plays one you have not.

You do not know who I am. You do not know who I am. A domain we have shared for millennia, and one I can share no longer. It is time. The time of the piper, the time of the question, the time of the forgetting. Only and only.

You are the.

The ode to balances (your shoulders see-sawing . . .
umhmmmMMmmm . . . their function) and the balance
which balances the balance, a shattering, your function, the
balancing of balances. The sway, the utter dismay in your
eyes. Sing! my love through the axes of your muscled eyes.

She did leave. She swam. Cross a pond. She gulped full her
lungs of air and spired wide her frightened eyes. And she
fanned atop the careening fleshy tips of the bottom to fund
me some words. Her sum words. "Give Love" a beg,
command, whispered joy, enactment, ideal, expectation,
truth, desire, symbol function sign, treasure, curse beginning
feeding slum, absence absence, flee of did she leave. O God,
can you be here, when she says give love. O. On give. I've
given. Veiled and. Silent is. My love.

Tell me, why do we speak?

He is old and his fingers shake like divining rods as they reach
to touch the earth. He moans and nods and turns and then he
walks away. Damp, he thinks, good and damp, damp enough.
He nods and stops and turns to find the coil of a wild yellow
rose aiming like an arrow at his heart. He is old and he visits.
He is old and he remembers the wild yellow roses his mother
asked for at her funeral. He was young and he remembers
looking into her closed face and he remembers her mouth
opening to ask "where are the roses?" He is old and they call
him rose man. They are young and think he is magic. He tells
them the only way to pick a rose is to grasp its stem firmly in
your palm, yanking blood from out its veins, he tells them
about respect. He is the rose man and he gives love and he is
the rose man and he waits for the piper to sing with him a
song, they burn with desire one for the other.

I am ready to die.

I am baptized by your words, they wet me and I am
confirmed. Pin me, unpin me, and hear these, my ugly
words, here, me failing, and hear me fail.

I know how little truth you tell me, I know how little you
tell me. You speak words.

(And) and I move toward my guitar who I know holds the
secret to an alleluia chorus that never ends . . .
Word, god, devil, let's me and you have a beer, Scotch (did
you know the top of hopscotch is heaven), let's me and you
skip a Scotch, have a beer.

Love . . . the greatest of all evils.

And when you least expect it the piper plays. And you look
for him and he looks for you, and a woman flips a card up
and demands a text. She desires meaning. Fashion yourself
being mean. Ask yourself what you want to happen. Ask.

Did you have almonds in your salad? The question behind
the question. Were the almonds slivered? Were raspberries
tossed in like blood drops? How many wedges of an orange
did you eat? Did the oranges come from China? Where
were you?

Forgive and forget me. Wet your lips once with your tongue.

The contrived part

This is where I long to be, in the body. Far away from the
beginning, far to go until the end. Slopping, tamping, racing
and camouflaging into the it.

His eyes are glazed and looking, obtuse for being within this
moment. And my hands (like a cup) let his jaw spill in and I
entice him forward into a kiss. I call him Heartstring.
Painted like the "c" on the harp, he demands to be struck.

For those who smoke, he is the lost flame, found and excited
with ignition. For those who don't, this is an other
expression of love.

I have nothing to hide, except my self.

I live inside the finite dwelling of the line
excised from the possibility of flourishes
disinheriting the potency
(your skin must taste of Mandarin oranges)
or of lichee nuts

did you not swim with them clutched in your hands across
an ocean for me?
your citrus fruits, like your drownings, bringing saliva to my
tongue

                                    He is building a scaffold of
words   in the summer
fallow. He carves   rock and
yellow birch

                        and cakes of straw and mud. He
                           whittles a word and he
sits it next   to the next, a side
by side, a series   of words. It
is June and as the sun   goes
down, its light shines through
     their spaces and he is building a
        paragraph to the sky. He is piling
           words, higher and higher, we read
              them, at dusk, by seeing the spaces
                 between them. And with the final
                    tangent of light all that is lit is the
                       bottom line, alone and burdened
                          by the wall on top of it.

And then I am on the train, missing the North Shore, missing you. I am in the dining car, watching rain attack the skylight, drinking Extra Old Stock, and a book is open in front of my ashtray. If the waiter changes my ashtray I might touch his artificial hand.

You talked once, about the reality of rain. You told me the possibilities of a spatial metaphor, you told me about the insatiable earth. But then again, you said the crowd pleaser was the blind-fold act. I remember every one of your lies.

The morning, and I am hungry for the newspaper, the crossword puzzle I never leave empty, the headlines never crossing my mind. The dining car is empty and the smell of coffee is sweet. The waiter sprinkles cinnamon into the froth of my café au lait and he jerks up his brow as if to ask me a question. I ask him about the possibility of a newspaper. He shakes his head and smiles as though he knew I might ask.

Out the window I am confirmed by the leaf of the mountain ash having turned blood red. No maple here, no diamond willow, no do-you-love-me buttercups. Just the jelling of xylem and the transformation of life into food.

Even the sky is ridiculous.

The charm

The sun, like a cell, a cello, divides and leaves us uncertain.
My face is copper, like a frieze or a coin. I am remote and
my lips are gently parted, I am the boy-head of a charm that
clinks and dangles from your wrist. You are my mother,
orange-eyed, emitting and silently magic.

I look up from my letter and the waiter is standing above
me. He smiles and asks if I would like another drink.

Two olives. The me/you olives inhaling the gin. I slide back
in my chair and cross my legs as I suck them from their
swords. The waiter walks away, pleased with his symbols. Of
course, I find him too abstract, too unwilling, too vague in
his flirtations. I fill my mouth with the martini and pick up
my pen.

I remember you always. You are a memory I have not
forgotten. You told me about perfection, about the riches of
the soul and you shared with me the reality of your losses.
Like a fog on a pond at sunrise you linger and hide and
collect and you are dispersed.

He brings me another drink. This time the olives are
speared by the same sword. He looks frantic and beat and his
eyes are unmoving but they tap dance. I look up to him and
say, what is it you are trying to say.

I asked him what it was he was trying to say. He is not at all like you. You I have never had to ask. When you shaved your head it took me weeks to notice. You, subtle as a metamorphosis. And the pleasure I took in asking who you were. Our lives together being blurred by the question mark.

I was tapped on my shoulder and reminded that time, moving, had acted like time. Cat Stevens says, trouble I haven't got a lot of time. Joni says this is a song for you, the piano being tapped as though soil were being brushed over the tops of transplants. I would like to forget this and plant us, our roots to entwine.

I have a confession. The screen across my window is not tight enough to keep out the rain. It is splashing across this page, begging us to once again belong to the world of the symbol, to the possibility of magic, to the other than. The place you told me where smoke pies live, where angels kiss faeries and where colours make sound. You gotta wanna clasp it like a stick bouncing off the skin of a snare drum. An ankle releasing a toe. Sssssssmp! Sssssssmp! The language is white and the camera drops to the dust left behind by the running away of your feet. And, I cannot tell you mmm when I need to sing. Mother, I am blind. The camera man's eyes have dilated, and to blink, he flicks his tongue across them.

I am in the dining car, dining, sipping a Scotch, tasting the transparency of rainbow trout, the sky is breathing heavily. The sky is combing its hair. So electric I thought I might die. So electric I thought I might never be the same having escaped it. And I miss rubbing cream into your skin. But a flock of night-hawks might be assembling in a basic poplar tree, and I might be missing the sight.

I remember. You brought me wild mushrooms, pollen bright on your sweating legs. And I remember we planted wild flowers in the rock garden. And the wasps we chanced upon stung shut our eyes. I remember the summer the birch bark turned red and the whisky-jacks ate from our hands. And I remember a fire blazing into your eyes, its reflection sparking in the spilling of your tears. And I rocked you, finally, in my arms.

You are a move away from me. I am travelling now, with a whisky spit with ginger and a smoke whose smoke curls into unbelievable question marks. Everything is utterly unbelievable, the way, at times, I need it to be. But it dawns on me, I am still calling for you to touch me. The waiter has loosened his tie and needs, although he won't, to sleep. This is a trip I have never taken, a going to I have never embarked upon, and yet I move as though a finger were tracing itself along the curve of a line; me, a dot upon it. A dot, upon it.

I suppose I should be perfectly honest.

You asked me once who I was. "Who are you?" you asked.

And then I am on the train and the meekness of twilight shatters in a riot of time and I am writing a poem in remembrance of you. And the poem is less than this. The poem is less than this. The poem, an attempt. The poem I write for you is unwritable. The poem I write for you must be spoken. The poem I write for you might be sung.

And you think this unwritability is something of an -ism, and yet, this is my only truth. You are a memory, an inscribable truth. Nothing greater than you can exist. And the train begins its widest curve. We are swinging as if we are a snapshot.

But of course, I am off track.

What it means to say "I love you like flowers love the rain"

I am in the hallway, moving toward you, my hands along the wall and the window steady me against the motion of the train. I am thinking what I might say to you when you open your cabin door, half naked, a whisky in your hand. Perhaps I will act naive and suppose a drink is what you had in mind. Perhaps the ash of your cigarette will drop away from your mouth and we will watch it fall. Perhaps you'll just call for me to come in. But what I knew would happen did and it happened as I thought it might. Or we will watch it tumble away.

We listen to the flesh of jazz, unaware it has ever begun. You tell me music is pretentious and that time is our only reality. You tell me that music exists only in its then. You are intoxicating me with words, you speak as though through a kaleidoscope.

           it is in my hand
    &   this is the line
             between life and death
      this is the line between "between"

here is the absolute absence of binary
with my tongue on your lip

sticking together like a whole
we are indivisible
this only is what is real

& when we sense it rolling across the floor you know I will go
you release me into the rain, the falling "it"

(my eyes will be searching in lamp-reflected panes)

or the self can be its own treacherous mirror

There are no mirrors in this small space, you have stolen
them all and you keep them hidden in a drawer of your
mahogany bureau. I am left with my tiny window or the
skylight, rain like lead pelting against them, to be the
remembrance of me. Or if the ice stays, I will see myself as I
sip.

Prelude & Fugue in D Major

Yes. I was thinking (my love) that I can see. You
are still-life like a snapshot and a tambourine is struck
on the palm of your hand
high, high above your head. And your eyes are bright like suns
and they have burned away their lids and they are lit
with the bowing of your head, because you love me and because
you are silent and because
ribbons of gold and red and green storm like

[for you I will dislodge
the sun from the sky]

purple around you and caress your warm and pale arms,
arms (webbing the air) as vacant as desire
to dance, as though you wish to be.
And all about you.
The background is blue. Blue or the sun . . . blue or the sun reflecting or
reflecting or refracting the panels   refracting the panels broken in the
broken in the wing (a window, petals like a rose: wing of a dragonfly

call it the rose glass and suck from it the light   blue-black back blue . . .
before you receive the tincture of its blood
or the taste like kill) of a dragonfly's blue-black back. Blue.
And kneel if you must upon my back
sky and earth so immemorial.
You progress through me: (a march) (you marched) an echo
to look (look . . . look but see) like sound waves. Ripples. Bubbles.
And you have tasted

[your tongue coils outward and snaps at the sky]

the mellifluous tongue of god and, perhaps, you have kissed
the feet of Christ.

And. The power of your absence is obscene.

All that is left is the blatant sun.

[the power of silence

the extracted blood . . .]

53

And the sun is bright like your eyes.

Behind you gathers the water of all
[lakes and ponds & rivers
and seas]
all droplets of dew nestling above the roots of all blades of grass.

The sky must pour without you

and we lay naked our brick backs to this earth

our (mouths) gaped open and

[I will free you from suffering]

((quivering))). You must slice open the sky.

. . . a crystal is never clear, a body never shadowless and the memory of forgetting looms like a spectre, winged and poised for entrance into its myth. Scuffing its heels across the tops of words, tapping a cane between their spaces, dipping cupped hands into the coolness of apostrophe . . .

[desire (whisper the word) desire]
Love you like flowers
love the rain.

Do you understand that? And the tops of my words begin to crumble. And I (I) I shall write for you a poem.

&

will you rock on your knees   there you are   I am an eye
and braid my words   in your glorious tower   who has fed on the sun
will you comfort me   as the façade begins   hungrily like a beast
as they crumble into silt   to peel away   and I swim in the pools
     you leave behind

beneath me is what frightens you
a skeleton unlaughing his laugh   your mortality

let me praise you, my only one
and let our fingerprints unite

     I cry into this mud
     cracked lake bottom
(&) silence is a basin of raucous dust   as though to quench its thirst
     I see you walking toward me (&)
glowing behind your silhouette   the world is silent as you tip
     and let fall forth water from your pail
like an eclipse   we are at once alone and united
     and the sun blazes in noon like an icon

you clasp your sweaty arms across my belly
rocking together, we fall

(or)

the bird poem   the angel of forgetting   the wail of desire
the screech   the blare   the cry, the howl
the words   the roar   the wail of desiring

[whisper a word
speak and enter
me]

(and) . . .

the seduction of a buttercup being fanned below your chin   [show me your privates]
or the nectar of honeysuckle received in your throat   [I am whispering]
but for the grounding of the eyes of a black-eyed Susan [deep, rich paints]
like the dandelion's trace on your fingertips for mother [laughing in kitchen
windows]
into the scream of the storm of her old white eyes

(or the whistle of woodpeckered birch in autumn)

I hold my head in my hands
and I cry
because of it all
                    that we might live again
                    the burden of love
                    that we might live again
                    the burden of love
                    that we might live again

(and) we fail, like the poem, to be silent

to be and

to enter the texture (of love)
        my love, my only one, is to die

Look   here the words have no flesh and their blood well is dry
        or we may dream the fossilled marrow of love's archaic bones
        [or of her ghost] homeless and searching [or of her ghost]
                and I have seen you caress her
            have heard her moan with ecstasy as she entered you
        for a moment

                        to sip on your senses
                    to dance with blood
                        gurgling in the tongue

        the wind will blow where it wills
        ah, perhaps the wind will whistle   [a burial]

Postlude

I was thrown off, pushed, from the train. I landed in a tiny clearing. And near midnight I heard the commotion of flowers. I tried to sneak away but soon their leaves and stems caught hold of me, tugging me into their procession.

You are called the name whose voice transcends the duplicity between the written and the spoken. You are cool fire. The one I long to plunge into. I will kingfish your soul. I will race through your field of sunflowers at midnight and stretch forth my lips to kiss the chalky surface of the waxing moon, the screaming moon. I will leave on the stoop of your porch a basket of freshly cropped foods, a bouquet of the wildest of wild roses, a pool of blood and the tooth from which it flowed. I will have you know the elements of which my desire is made real.

To invent the event of love is to remove
from you that descent into the utterance

speaking spirals and spools
wind me up in your web of words

entrap me like a net, let me breathe again
the invisible symbol of beginning

again to ache for the illusion of liberation
comes to me in a dance of solitude utter

solitude in dance it comes to me like sun fire
boils my blood burns my hair bloats my body

explodes into fragments innumerable and I scatter
to the floor of the earth and wait to be thrown
like a stone to the sea or over the shoulder my love
like a stone to the sea or over your shoulder my love

The morning we were diving from cliffs, you told me of a dream you dreamed. You said you dreamed you had lost your memory. And as I threw myself like a swan from the edge, I wondered how this dream of yours was possible. And as I entered the wave front in a froth I thought how problematic you make my life.

For breakfast we ate steak and eggs, drank chicken broth from coffee mugs, sweetened our breath with watermelon and honeydew, drank a glass of white wine and made love in the shadows of a crevice of a cave. And when I awoke to the mid-afternoon sun, you greeted me with a knife blade and an oyster. And as I took it into my mouth you fantasized about sending the knife through the back of my neck. Quick, sharp motions have often been your passion.

once again, for you . . .

and perhaps you will be holding up the front of your shirt
within which you collect the acrobatic blossoms of an
ancient orange tree and perhaps we have mistaken them for
butterflies spinning in your hair and perhaps I might lick the
underside of your chin mistaking a love song for uneaten
honey and then perhaps when we die we become stars

I was thinking (I am silent) that your absence is power. And then how I wished I would fall asleep in a grove next to a brook and dream of the love we might make. But instead I remembered how relative things have become; how utterly disinterested I am to your denying me.

And then, of course, we are neither here nor there. We are across the table, sharing coffee. And you ask me "what does falling have to do with love?" I want to say that falling is the absence of love, but instead I nudge my foot closer to yours.

We fall like orange blossoms in a glass cage, and die looking coveting the honey bee's nectar-soaked limbs. But all this, of course, tells you I am off the train. Planted. And here I am enticing you to revolutionize the language of love.

But here is a simple reminder of what took place:

The word "love" entered our discourse, our feet met (whether yours was propelled toward mine I do not know) and then we danced with tongues. The cross you wear around your neck, speaking to me, silencing me, challenging me, sinning me.

Sin.

A timeless word, begot, not made, before all worlds. But what does falling have to do with sin?

(s)word
si(g)n

Irises

The pigment in my irises has dulled, sunlight so elusive, sunlight so grand. Sprung. Enduring. Somehow. Remembering to breathe. Lungs change the colour of blood (pockets of oxygen fondling, straining to tickle, to tempt).

And I remember Michael slaying the serpent, keeping evil at bay. His sword is raised, heaven bent and flaming.

The semen splashes onto my belly, a nipple, into my hair, onto the corner of my mouth. I lick it away, my chest heaving, I fall into sleep, dreaming of spiders' webs, of the heart in a moth's chalky skin exploding.

I prefer it this way—a generous monasticism, a profusion of solitude—not a dark night, but a bright, windy day of the soul.

That summer the black flies were exceptionally bad. We didn't even worry how cold the water was. We just dove in.

Chokecherry pie on
chipped yellow plate on
stoop & sweet
iced tea on
mother's warm knee
rests my neck
fingers swarming
my hair
(she dreams, permanent waves)
white from sunlight
her hand swipes
a mosquito flies
away, sideways
shoulders are speckled eggs
hot from the day at the dock
bumpy from bug bites
stones I skipped still
fluttering, fearing
that final (clack) across a rock
her mossy cheek slashed

No wonder, ancients intensely terrified of the moon
eclipsing the sun, northern nomads punished in months of
darkness, running, returning (looking for light) like a crow.
Throwing her pinion, oily and smooth, rowing her wing
purple, slipping feathers from her breast, her tail, one by
one, her black beak whittling, blood feathers falling,
shapings for (nests). Her quills, quickly forgotten.

But I have turned the crusted earth, picked off a scab,
watched it, felt it, smelled it bleed. I smelled it bleed.

> trumpet fanfares, toccatas
> fuguettes, the titmouse &
> whistling whisky-jacks
> wild rhubarb, bright water
> sky & rocks, musty cedars
> sweeping shore, mergansers

The milk man, being hung over, has spilled milk in a mud puddle. A rainbow blooms from a dripping oil pan.

If truth be spoke, I am missing you, both index fingers, my foreskin and the French Open. I struggle with metaphysics, I have a severe attitude, I am intensely narcissistic.

I have some records I am proud of. I once sneezed seventeen times in a row while staring into the sun. I have had eleven orgasms in one day. I have had a six minute love affair. I have had three visions of the divine. I have read every published word of an author you have never heard of. I have drunk Robert Kroetsch under the table. I have been in love twice.

Mother and I were blind drunk on dandelion wine. She said call me Dorris. I played for her the guitar, sang a song I said I wrote. We were at the cottage. The windows were wide and open, crickets were picking up where loons were leaving off, finally our feet began to cool. She said I'm magic you know. The sound and smell of water rose like yellow roses, petals falling, spinning, catching, being caught. Our Irish setter stretched and turned at the foot of the screen door. A fire lit itself, birch bark crackling. On the mantle sat a tiny birch bark canoe, a wind-up bonging clock, a whittled diamond willow dog, a green glass ashtray full of pins and dust and wayward marbles. We had cigarettes to smoke. The creaks of a spring, the slap lap ping of a screen door.

These are the generations of the heavens

singing wings dawn's icons cold as stone
at the instant reds flare into blue, blood being heaved
through her womb

and they shall be turned to blood
stones, feathers, brothers, wine
tumbling like dark sky strung
a faggot snaps beneath your feet
begin to burn

but they shall not be burnt on the altar for a sweet savour
savior sweet, tiara of thyme, taste the salt in your armpits
tell no story like the trace of white wine and sweet basil
snipped into the smiling sauce bubbling over and laughing
we make love with the curtains drawn

we found the men that gathered sticks
and wove them into crowns to burn

and that prophet, or that dreamer of dreams
he can see beds laughing, pond scum blackening
the surface above him, military tanks pointing guns
never engaging in a rush in a hush washed of night
mares standing still to suckle standing still to sleep

Shall we sense the meaninglessness of this flow, or shall we
lose it? Why don't we gather irises? Yes. By the Red River
they must grow. Wild irises. Must grow wild. Cupped to
catch the rain. They clasp together their shaking palms, they
worship the potential of words.

They rise up and go a whoring after the gods, somersaulting
themselves into absence divine, doubling in the fields,
doubled in the sky, squinting stamens in wind storm, petals
like lids.

                                                    She tends to kiss
my nose with the opening and closing of her eyelashes.

                              She calls them angel kisses.

She takes me, hides me, lowers me through the window. Barn swallows watch as I slip through the dawning of a crescent moon and into a labyrinth of corn fields. The corn is cold, not yet wet with dew. I am hot on the trail of a poem.

I met him in the middle of night. He had been gnawing on raw cobs of corn, snapping together his teeth. Strands of silk decorate the earth, black and moist, a breathing burn. He heard me thrashing through the stalks toward him. O yes, raised his eyes into mine. He wipes his mouth with the palm of his hand. I stopped. We stared. He continued to eat. He motions me to sit. The earth is cool on my skin. I noticed his hands, scraped and blood-stuck dried. Noticed me noticing. His hair was long, dusty, skin is deeply tanned. His clothing, new but soiled. His feet are bare. I snapped off and shucked an ear of corn. That was before. We ate in silence and slept in one another's arms. At morning we answered the call of a bird, bathed in his stream, ate raspberries but walked westward through a forest of firs. He ground faces of gods across pine needles and sand with a sapling's branch. I read his drawings like dreams.

Then I kissed him, and he lifted up his voice, and wept. As though language were death, beautifully once, oval, sound-proof.

Did I ever promise you the unmistakable discovery of origins?

Your eye sockets are window boxes, stuffed full with flowers. Sunflower, quaking grass, just Joey, lobelia.

On the clothesline in your backyard sits the Red Sacred Swallow. Legend has it that her red throat is a reminder that she has pulled a thorn from Christ's crown as he hung (defunct) on the cross. She remembers how he saw his reflection in the brimming grail, how he whispered to himself, "this is my blood." She remembers his astounded eyes.

At his tomb
she drops
from the sky
winged everlasting, scarlet
pimpernel, Humboldt's sunray, pink
poker statice, purple
groundsel, ruby
grass, cupid's heart,
stardust, a bush
of wild rose and
the petals of Mexican tulip
poppies.
She heaps a prairie
dome, en-nested a tomb
sky registers under
her wings
fly away
leaf-like and petal
over head stones

I sing the hymn of forgetting
the song of mother's quilt in spring time, covering my face
of soft skin on samplers, sun-dried sheets
sleep so easy like sorcery

And I want to wake from my dream but not to wake
to do the one two cross, three four criss like she can do
& stay here, between stitches
shining arabesques

Big-eyed needles and green-ended pins stick out her tightly
pursed lips though she had a story to tell. Front of her sits a
frame full of double nine patch, taut and forgiving. Punches
the needle through. Fabric vibrates for an instant, breathes.
Three, four stitches at a time, pulls thread through and
under, up. She lifts her eyes to the whisky-jacks on the flat,
simply wrought feeder. Costco has sunflower seeds on sale
next week. She looks for the flyer, pins it to the fridge.

But you must remember the tomb would be empty, a stone rolled away, a village crushed under its weight. Her flowers, her mound of flowers, sensuous & swept by the wind away from and into (a random fall of ash) the tomb. When the rock rolled away, she had nothing to say. Still, she plucks the blossoms, flies high, releases her catch. Soon the sun himself will be obscured. Sweet hillock, oozing with life, born so dumbly.

And there came a man of God, or so he said. He was a handsome man, no one could deny it. His beard, turning some grey, was neatly trimmed. His eyes were cobalt, they splintered and sprayed. His hair was a very light brown, almost blond, going grey, about to thin. His hands were tanned, big, veined, a light streak of hair crossed his knuckles, it shone in the sunlight. I have seen them before, on a train running east. He was wearing a finely tailored suit, double breasted, summer wool. His shoes and belt and nails shone, highly buffed. His lips were dry and healthy, the colour of a tangerine. He sat with his legs crossed, sipping something on ice from a highball. He had no nose.

And besides, from his irises sprung the wild and chanting blueflag, petalled pupils, their blooms reaching to the sky (like opened mouths) in wanton abandonment. Long, thin stalks protruding to feel or taste the falling feathers of angels' wings. The heavy buds bobbing as if to touch you. No one seemed to notice except to say "how beautiful."

There there sweet baby

(cup your hands, catch the rain)
pistil-joined
ovary,
progress throughout me
Chinese dragon
slayer of the sun, tattooed to the moon
make us gods or fools
jestering through sky-tall fields
of sunflowers kissing

There there sweet baby
eat the flesh
drink the blood
of an orange
I will decorate your eyes
with the dye

Inimitable rhapsodies: none like sunlight wrapping her arms
around you at last

Torenia: the "wishbone plant."
Inside the bloom is a small ridge
shaped just like . . .

we walk on broken bones
                              all these broken bones
                        say, walk away
      say sweet baby walk away

I think the clouds are your lungs. Not a question of 'do I
love you?' Maybe I just need one more drink. Or I need to
walk under the night sky (the moon is clouded out with the
stars). I need to feel that cold breeze washing up my pant
legs. To smell the dirt moving in the Assiniboine. Taste the
Coke can weeds, swallow the undertow.

The long expected electric light made its appearance on Main Street on the night of October 15th, 1882. Three lights being in operation, one at the corner of Broadway and Main, one in front of the Imperial Bank, near Post Office Street, and one at the C.P.R. Depot. The light Factory was located at the H.B. mill, near the mouth of the Assiniboine.

We used to walk by that river, under hundreds of lights shaded by twisted trees, down a footpath. You would carry me over a piss-bruised bush and lay me on the damp undergrowth. The Golden Boy waved his ass in my eyes. You'd say how you relish the taste of tobacco on my lips. My head would roll to and fro as though I wanted to elude your touch. In the morning I will look into the mirror and wonder how it is I see your reflection there. Glass on polished lead, almost like a dream of beginnings. Hell, we might even construct a history from it all.

Instead, every time I think of you I clasp a weighted leather thong around the top of my scrotum, stretching the flesh back into foreskin. I want everything back, especially the northeast corner of my soul you have framed above your fireplace, colored like quickly flaring flames.

It has been too long for me to not be over you. But I was so far under . . .

Hundreds of small verses
by different hands
become one
habit of the unrequited.

—Michael Ondaatje